TABLE OF CONTENTS

Page

Introduction 1

The Time Sensitive Targeting Dilemma 2

The Limits of Technology 4

The OODA Loop" 6

The Current State of TSTs 7

The Future of TST 11

Operation HURRICANE 12

Conclusion 14

Endnotes 16

Bibliography 17

Introduction.

Time Sensitive Targeting or TST has emerged as a buzz phrase in recent conflicts. Technology in the form of computers, high speed communications systems, precision guided munitions, and improved intelligence, surveillance, and reconnaissance (ISR) systems offer great promise in the effort to prosecute important emerging targets in the fastest manner possible. Given the advances in technology, senior leaders have come to expect the time period from detection to engagement of a TST will decrease as a function of the technology. In fact, General John Jumper, the current Chief of Staff of the United States Air Force (USAF) believes that the USAF should be able to manage the TST problem from sensor (detection), to strike, in single digit minutes[1]. However, technology is only part of the equation and does not address an even more important aspect of striking important time critical targets. An analysis of the current state of TST prosecution will show that technology can only go so far and we are rapidly approaching the point of diminishing returns from technological advances. An honest look at the problem shows the key to increasing the speed with which TSTs are engaged is a multi-faceted problem that requires work in three key areas. First, technological innovation can continue to shorten the time it take to acquire, confirm, and engage TSTs. Second, the problem requires a change in acceptance by senior civilian leadership that allows TSTs to be engaged decisively. Finally, the problem requires the development of joint doctrine that defines how the Untied States military will manage this capability in the future.

The Time Sensitive Targeting Dilemma.

Carl von Clausewitz said "war is an extension of politics"[2] and that remains just as true today as when he wrote this axiom 150 years ago. Of equal importance to the problem of striking TSTs are the political considerations that arise in situations involving high-profile

1

targets. Often, TSTs are located in areas that may inflict substantial collateral damage to people and materials located in the vicinity of the target. In the case of collateral damage against civilians, the results of such an attack may be of greater harm than allowing the TST to continue to function. Take for example the F-117 strike on the Al Firdos bunker during Operation Desert Storm[3]. U.S. intelligence thought the bunker was serving as a command post and recommended the strike. Unfortunately the bunker was also in use as a shelter for civilians and the nighttime raid killed more than one hundred women and children. Examples of the two most likely TSTs illustrate the true scope of the collateral damage problem. Imagine a Weapons of Mass Destruction (WMD) storage site containing chemical munitions is detected near an enemy population center. While destroying enemy WMD capabilities may be vital to the interests of the United States and our allies, the secondary effects of striking a storage site on the surrounding population must be taken into account. Attacking the WMD prevents the application of those weapons against friendly forces. However, striking the WMD site may also spread deadly material causing injury and death to any non-combatants within a radius of the site. The damage inflicted on civilians in the local area may turn the tide of public support for the conflict and do more damage to the long-term outcome of the conflict.

In a second scenario, imagine a high-level leadership target is located in the enemy capitol. Next to the target location is the embassy of a neutral government that has a vote on the United Nations Security Council. While it may be possible to immediately target and eliminate the leadership target, in doing so it is highly possible damage will be inflicted on buildings surrounding the target. While the benefit of removing enemy leadership is apparent, the political ramifications of damage to the neutral country embassy or neutral country deaths may well prove more dangerous to the overall situation.

As both of these scenarios demonstrate, precision guided munitions and the technology inherent to the TST capability present a double-edged sword. Clearly, modern weapons are so lethal that the possibility of first, second, and third order effects must be examined in all situations. What is strikingly clear is that senior leaders are often faced with a dilemma when trying to decide whether or not to strike a TST. Naturally, senior leadership is going to react by becoming involved in the process. As a result, the Department of Defense (DOD) needs to devote serious effort to developing a model that will guide senior leaders, tactical commanders, and the warrior at the tip of the spear.

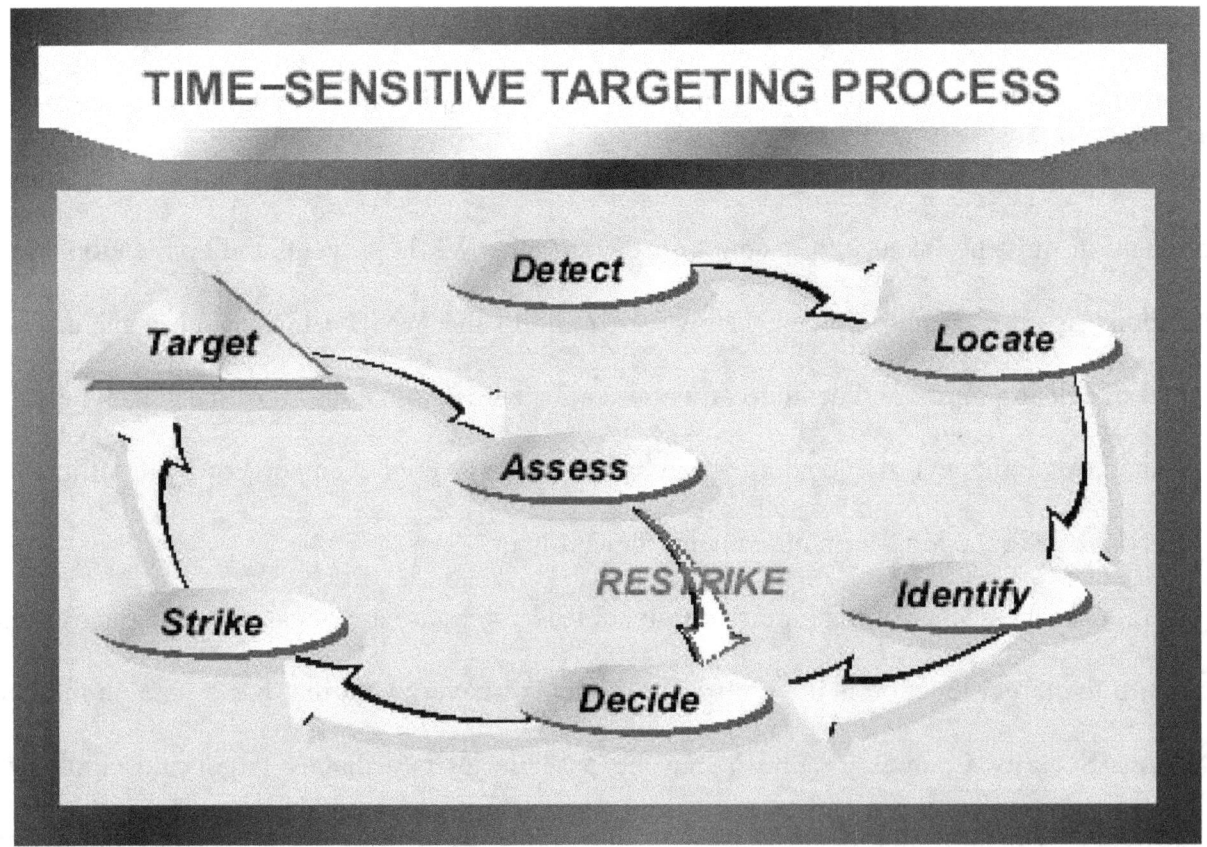

Figure 1.

The concept for the Time-Sensitive Targeting Process as currently outlined in the Commander's Handbook for Joint Time-Sensitive Targeting is straightforward and depicted in Figure 1. However, it is important to note that this document, published by United States Joint

Forces Command, is not doctrine. In fact, there is no current DOD doctrine for managing and prosecuting TSTs. Currently, United States European Command, United States Central Command, and United States Forces Korea each use a separate set of processes and tools to conduct TST operations within their theater.[4] While cooperation on TST operations between the USAF, USMC, USN, and USA has been excellent, there has been no overall attempt to standardize the process between the services and the Combatant Commands.

While the lack of doctrine might seem to be a major problem, there is an even bigger problem that is becoming more and more obvious. In the past senior leaders gave direction to military commanders and expected that guidance to be carried out within the boundaries of the rules of engagement. Over the past 25 years the USAF championed this strategy with the phrase "centralized control, decentralized execution."[5] Central to the this theme was the belief that senior level commanders would give guidance based on the political concerns and the overall strategy of a problem while enabling the on-scene military person to decide the best way to accomplish the mission. From the USAF perspective it allowed the pilot in the aircraft to determine the best method for attacking a target given the conditions he or she was encountering at the moment of attack. In the bigger picture, it kept senior level commanders out of the cockpit so the commander on the scene could prosecute the target without undue influence that might serve to endanger the pilot or other U.S. forces on the ground.

The Limits of Technology.

With the advance of technology, the concept of decentralized execution no longer holds true. As a result mainly of off-board video systems, which send sensor imagery over data-link or satellite communications in real time and the Common Operating Picture (COP), and displays the real-time position of all friendly units in the battlespace on a single map, it is now possible to send a live display of the battle from the perspective of the ground, from the air, or from space, to any location on earth. While the capability was designed to send the imagery to ground teams or decision makers in the CAOC, it has now found it's way to Combatant Commander's Headquarters, the Pentagon, and even the White House. As a result, the volume of and fidelity of information presented to commanders and civilian leadership creates a situation where everyone gets a vote in the process. Additionally, elevating tactical information to the strategic level can have several unintended consequences. While bringing senior leadership into the TST process insures the overall goals of the nation are compiled as part of the military calculus, it also adds a layer of review that may slow the process. Obviously slowing the process not only goes against the concept of TST, it also goes against another construct that has evolved in the military establishment in recent years, the OODA loop.

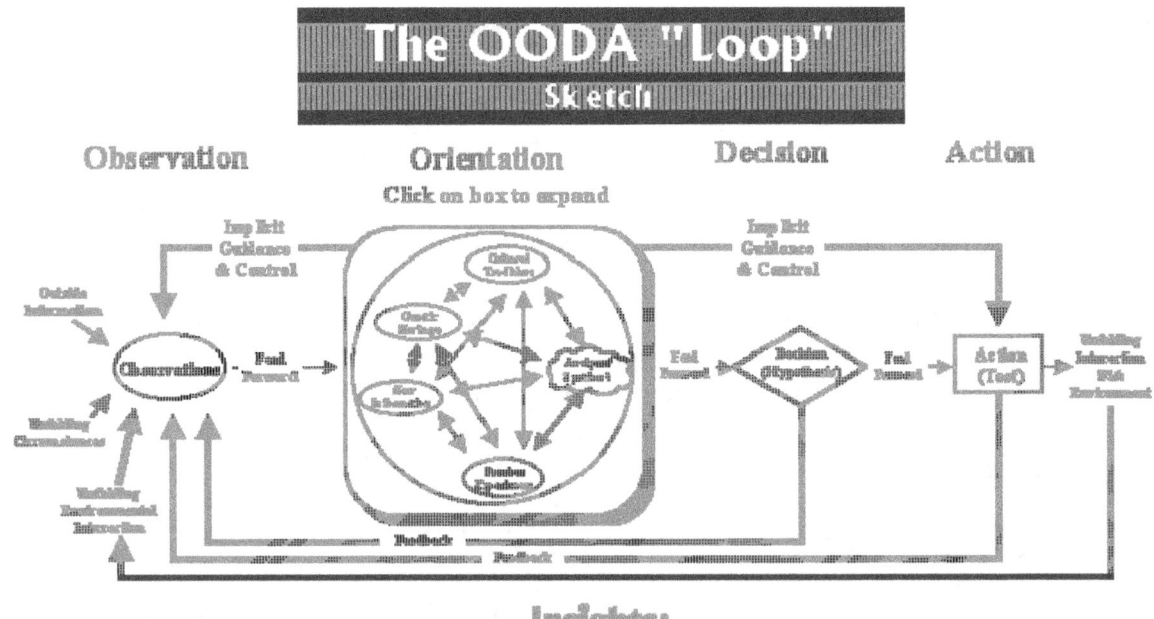

Figure 2.

The OODA LOOP.

In the mid 1970's a USAF fighter pilot named John Boyd developed a concept for understanding how decisions are made. His OODA loop concept stands for Observation, Orientation, Decision, Action and can be described as a model that provides a framework for understanding how decisions are made. The model, illustrated in figure 2, is central to the concept of TST. The basic premise of the OODA loop is that by understanding how decisions are made, it is possible to speed the process and make decisions faster than your adversary.

Once you accelerate your decision process to a rate faster then the adversary you are said to be inside his OODA loop and you can make decisions that he cannot react to, which will ultimately allow you to position yourself for victory.

Technology is accelerating our capability within the OODA loop construct, in fact, three sections of the OODA loop construct are directly improved by recent advances. The Observation phase has been improved through better ISR systems which provide better fidelity on the enemy, the Orientation phase, arguably the most important, has been improved through C3I systems enhancements which allow U.S. commanders to rapidly position and arrange forces on the battlefield, and finally the Action phase has seen rapid improvement through the growth of precision guided munitions which can strike nearly any spot on earth with pin-point accuracy.

On the surface it would appear that technology has made it possible for the U.S. to run a faster OODA loop than any of our potential adversaries. Unfortunately, all of the advances in the other three phases of the OODA Loop have been offset by a slowdown in the Decision phase[6]. As senior level leadership has inserted itself in the cockpit it is in fact creating a friction point that must be addressed to truly get the most out of technology and the system. To emphasize this point one need look no further than a recent comment from the surface track coordinator for the TST currently working operation OIF, "We might get someone tapping us on the shoulder saying, "I just got a phone call from back in the United States, and they want (a certain location) targeted in 45 minutes.""[7] To some this seems like throw back to the Vietnam War when President Johnson insisted on managing the targeting process personally over breakfast.[8] To others it is simply an effort by senior leadership to ensure the strategic implications of an attack are taken into account.

The Current State of TSTs.

Recent examples illustrate that while we have come a long way in our capability to prosecute TSTs, we still have a ways to go. Perhaps the most enlightening example occurred on the first night of Operation Enduring Freedom (OEF). As the attacks were beginning, an unmanned aerial vehicle (UAV) called Predator located a convoy containing what was thought to be the leader of the Taliban Mullah Muhammad Omar and tracked it to a building.[9] The Predator flying that night was a new variety that is armed with two AGM-114 Hellfire missiles. The TST cell initiated procedures to attack this target and senior leadership at United States Central Command (CENTCOM), was notified. On duty at CENTCOM that night was a U.S. Navy Judge Advocate General (JAG), officer whose job was to provide legal opinion about law of armed conflict, proportionality, and international law to the commander. In this case, the on duty JAG determined that there were several problems with targeting the building with a Hellfire missile. The JAG questioned the proportionality of using a Hellfire missile to strike a person. Additionally, he pointed out that the hellfire as a weapon had never been vetted as an acceptable means of attacking anything other than a military target. In this case the JAG refused to authorize the strike, which led to discussions as to whether the JAG actually had the authority to authorize or deny the attack. While the discussion continued at CENTCOM and the CAOC, Omar was able to escape.[10] This event was not an isolated case, a report by the Washington Post found that on numerous occasions pilots were unable to strike senior Taliban and Al-Qaeda leadership targets.[11] Clearly this example demonstrates that the process must be changed and there has to be political buy-in if we hope to get the most out of the TST capability.

While the previous example shows the leadership issues associated with TSTs, there is another important aspect that needs to be addressed, the limits of technology. One of the real lessons to come from OIF is the realization that technology will not solve all of the problems with TST. Moore's Law states that the speed of computers will double every eighteen months[12], but improvements in processing power will cannot overcome the basic laws of physics and it still takes time to cover the distance from point one point to another in the battlespace. The speed of current aircraft and missile systems means that in order to prosecute TSTs, a suitable platform must be nearby. Since the time and place a TST will emerge cannot be predicted, this capability must be present in the battlespace 24 hours a day during a conflict. Modern aircraft and missiles are faster than they have ever been but it still takes time to load an aircraft with the correct munition, program a cruise missile, coordinate for tanker and electronic warfare support for a strike package, and ultimately to fly from point A to point B. Additionally, they must have the fuel and support needed to accomplish the strike. In fact, the single biggest limiting factor in striking TSTs with airborne assets during OIF was availability of airborne gas or tanker support.[13]

Operation Iraqi Freedom (OIF) provides the most up to date example of the TST process and the limitations of technology. While the process was somewhat complex as depicted in figure 3, it was actually very efficient. During OIF TSTs were separated into three distinct categories Terrorist, Leadership, and WMD.[14] Even though the scope of TSTs was limited to these three categories, there were 156 separate TSTs operations conducted during OIF.[15] Of those approximately 95% received approval in less than two minutes.[16] While that sounds efficient, it is the details of the other 5% that reveal the true limitations of TST.

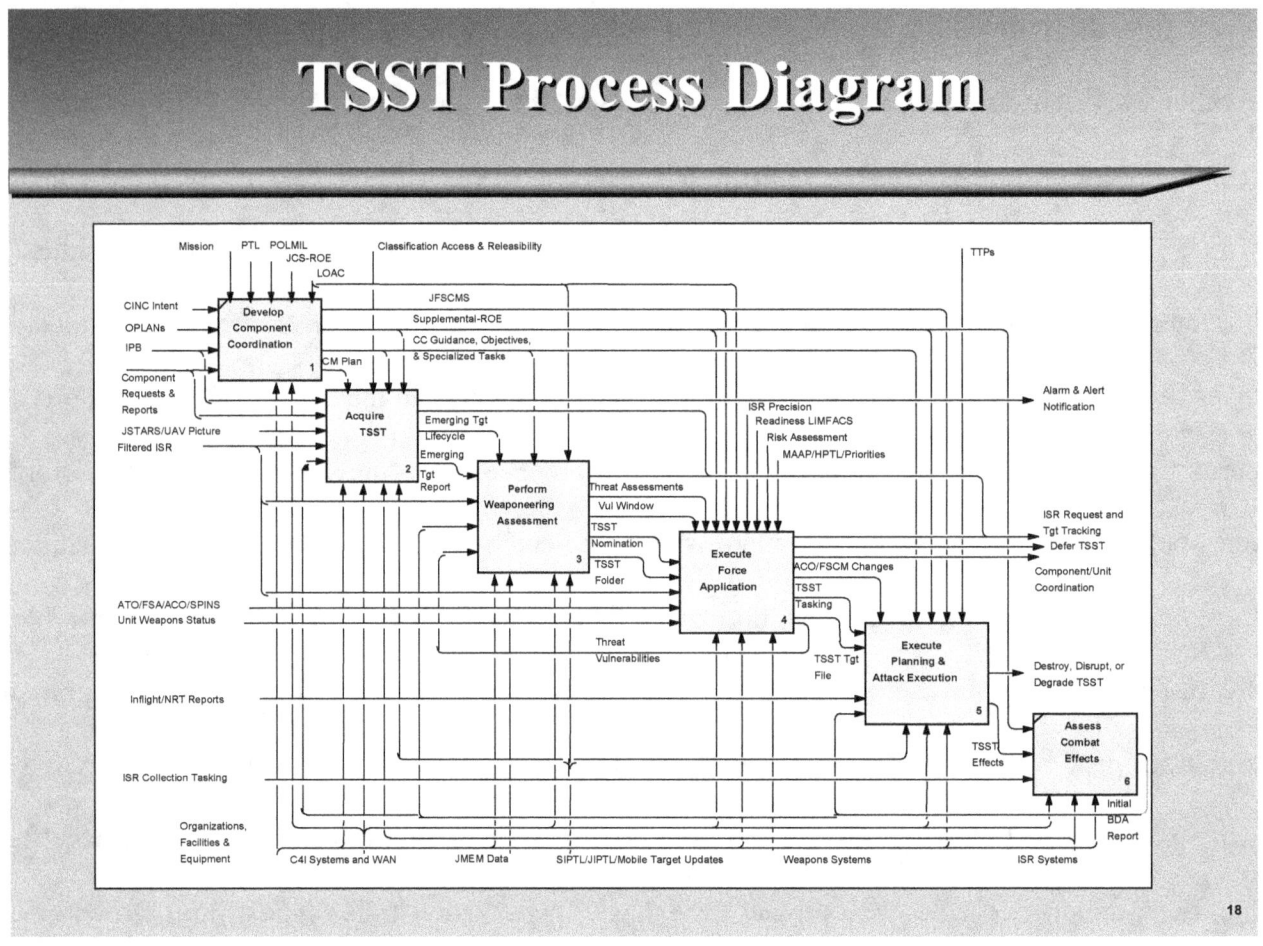

Figure 3.

The first strike TST strike of OIF demonstrates some of the time and space problems associated with TSTs. This strike came about as a result of information that Saddam Hussein was spotted entering a bunker complex. The information was provided by other governmental agencies (OGAs), and was thought to have a high degree of reliability. What complicated this attack was the fact that the war had not actually started, in fact, the opening strike of the war was scheduled to take place the following night. It took approximately 2 1/2 hours to get approval for the strike and planning commenced to put together a strike on the bunker. Two F-117's were rearmed with two GBU-27 laser guided bombs each. These bombs are highly accurate and are designed to penetrate hardened targets. Additionally, 40 Tomahawk land attack cruise missiles were targeted against the bunker. It then took several hours for the aircraft and cruise missiles to make their way to the bunker. Ultimately, the strike failed and Saddam was not killed in the attack.[17] Debate continues as to whether there was actually a bunker in the specified location, but the important lesson to take away is the extended period of time required to strike this TST was a function of speed of the attacking weapons systems sent to hit the bunker.

It is a common mistake to assume that if a target emerges you can simply send a plane to bomb it. The reality is typical TST strike aircraft such as the B-2, F-117, and F-15E need support in the form of tankers to provide gas to make it to the target and back, electronic warfare support to jam enemy surface to air missiles systems, air support to remove the threat of enemy fighters, and ISR support to maintain contact with the target and provide assessment after the strike. All of which must be coordinated and synchronized throughout the attack.

Clearly the problems associated with the current construct for TST are complex and there are no easy answers that will solve all of the problems. However, the future of TST will likely include changes that will smooth the process and lay a foundation for developing a better understanding of the method and processes for rapidly striking emerging targets on the battlefield. Improving the speed and effectiveness of the TST mechanism in the future will require the use of doctrinal, political, and technological innovation.

The first step to solving the TST problem and making it more effective for the future is the establishment of doctrine that provides an overarching guide and standardizes the process across the Department of Defense. Doctrine must be developed that captures and defines the process across all services and combatant components. This doctrine should outline a universal process for identifying, vetting, targeting, and assessing the important targets that emerge in the battlespace. The development of doctrine is often viewed as a painful process of putting common sense on paper, but it is absolutely necessary to ensure the U.S. conducts military operations in the most effective manor.

The Future of TST

The next step for developing the future of TST is critical to the future of TST, political "Buy-In". Senior civilian and military leaders must always remain a key part of the TST process, because ultimately they must bear responsibility for the actions of the nation's military. However, we should at least make an attempt to return to the concept of centralized control, decentralized execution. In order to make this happen it will require a certain amount of effort from both senior leaders and military operators. Senior leaders must work to develop trust in the process and the people controlling the process. This goal can be accomplished by deliberate planning and discussion about the types of targets and situations that may develop during a conflict. Likewise military operators can increase cooperation by anticipating likely decision points that will face senior leaders and preparing for those occurrences.

The final step to improving the future of TST is the development of technology and tactics that will get the most out of the TST process. The last ten years have seen an explosion in the number and capability of precision guided weapons. The U.S. must continue efforts to make munitions smarter and more capable. In order to get the most out of these developments, the construct of TST should become a part of the munition development process. Instead of developing technology for technology's sake, the U.S. should focus efforts and develop munitions that give commanders more flexibility in explosive yield, controllability, and assessment. Eventually the U.S. may need the capability to strike TSTs that are beyond the traditional terrestrial boundaries. In order to prepare for that future we must focus our technological advancement now.

One potential method for dealing with the doctrinal, political, and technological aspects of prosecuting TSTs involves pre-approval and discussion before the actual conflict begins, as well as the use of data-linked weapons that can be launched then maintained in an undetected location near the potential target. Under this construct senior Department of Defense leadership would present a list of the top five TSTs to senior civilian leadership for discussion and approval. Limiting the list to the five most important TSTs would help keep focus and encourage detailed discussion to reduce decision time should one emerge during the battle. Once the list was scrubbed and approved, authority for initial engagement would be delegated to the theatre agency responsible for managing TSTs. If one of the five targets emerges the TST cell would have the option of launching a data-linked weapon that would proceed to the target area. As with most conflicts, there are variables that cannot always be accounted for. Using this construct, the TST cell has the ability to funnel decision making to whatever level is necessary, while guiding the weapon to the target area, then placing it in an undetected holding area while the senior leaders make a final decision to attack the TST. If approval comes through the weapon is in very close proximity and can immediately engage the target. If approval is denied, the data-linked weapon can then be steered to a dump target where it will do no harm. An illustration of the above model is demonstrated with the following fictional scenario.

OPERATION HURRICANE.

The United States has responded to a major state that is threatening to destabilize a region. A coalition force was formed to force regime change as well as remove the state's capability to produce and employ WMD. Before the conflict began, the Combatant Commander submitted his top five TST targets to the NCA for approval. The list included the dictator of the rogue state, WMD employment platforms, mobile WMD production platforms, the rogue state's equivalent of Secretary of Defense, and mobile double digit surface to air missile systems (SAMs). In this case, the Combined Air Operations center (CAOC) has the preponderance of assets as well the ability to command and control the process, so they have been designated the controlling authority for managing TST engagements. Senior leadership reviewed the list and approved initial engagement on the top five targets with the following restrictions: All targets may be attacked if there will be less than 30 collateral damage deaths. Weapons may be launched to hold points if there will be more than 30 collateral damage deaths, potential damage to third country structures or personnel, or possible release of WMD.

Once combat operations begin ISR assets discover the potential location of the dictator and the TST cell activates an attack on the target. The Combined Forces Air Component Commander (CFACC) is on the floor of the CAOC and begins to process the incoming information. The TST cell determines through two sources that the dictator is indeed in the specified location with a high degree of certainty. An initial examination of the target location determines there is a restaurant and shopping complex nearby. The TST cell in consultation with the CFACC determines that the target is valid but there is the potential for more than 30 collateral damage deaths. Using the new model the CFACC is able to approve the launch of two data-linked JSAAM missiles that are given a hold point 10 miles from the target. The CFACC is then able to initiate contact with the NCA to notify them of the situation and seek final approval for the attack. While the discussion takes place at the NCA level, both of the JASSM missiles navigate to the target area and set up a hold profile unnoticed by the hostile forces due to their stealth capability. After several minutes of discussion the decision is made and approval is given to engage the target. The data is sent to the JASSM missiles and they accelerate out of their orbit point covering the 10 miles to the target in just over a minute. The missiles proceed to the target area and acquire the target with their sensors. The target imagery is confirmed by an assessment team in the CAOC and final approval is sent to the weapon. As the weapon dives into the target, weaponeering information is sent to the warhead and the munition is tuned to deliver just enough explosive yield to ensure the target is destroyed without causing excessive collateral damage.

While this version of the scenario ends with the destruction of the target, the decision process could have just as easily revealed a mosque that holds significant importance to a member of the coalition or public opinion. In this case striking the target will cause more collateral damage than the coalition is willing to accept. In this case the two JASSM missiles would be directed to another target or to a pre-selected dump area. In both cases the time period for the kill chain is reduced, there is more clarity of information being presented to the decision makers, and more importantly, senior leaders have more options without placing U.S. lives at risk.

Conclusion.

The future of TST is far from certain. Advances in technology in the form of sensors, guidance, and propulsion will allow senior commanders more and more lethal options for dealing with high priority targets. What is certain is that politics and public opinion will remain as important to the future of TST as technology. Accordingly, the Department of Defense should develop and implement TST doctrine now to make the most of this promising capability. Senior leadership should participate in the process and develop a construct for streamlining the process. Additionally, technology must be developed that gives commanders and strikers more flexibility when attacking TST. Finally, the DOD must continue to look to the future and anticipate the types of targets that our government may need to target in the future so the United States is prepared when the next call comes.

Notes

[1] Jumper, John, P., General, AFA National Symposia,
   http://new.aef.org/pub/Jumper2001.asp

[2] Clausewitz, Carl, *On War*

[3] Lambeth, Benjamin, S. *The Transformation of American Air Power,* Cornell Univerity Press, 2000.

[4] Commanders TST handbook, page iv..

[5] Colonel John G. Cronican, Jr.
   http://www.airpower.maxwell.af.mil/airchronicles/aureview/1981/jan-feb/cronican.htm#cronican

[6] Lambeth, Benjamin, Senior Staff member, Rand Corporation, Interviewed by author December 7, 2004

[7] http://public.afca.af.mil/Intercom/2003/june/09.html

[8] http://www.airforcehistory.hq.af.mil/PopTopics/vietnam.htm

[9] http://www.washingtonpost.com/ac2/wp-dyn?pagename=article&node=&contentId=A44546-2001Dec14&notFound=true

[10] Ibid

[11] Ibid

[12] http://www.intel.com/research/silicon/mooreslaw.htm

[13] Plentl, Brett, A, LtCol, USAF, Chief Time Sensitive Targeting Cell, Operation Iraqi Freedon, Interviewed by Author December 7, 2004.

[14] OIF by the numbers

[15] Ibid

[16] Plentl, Brett, A, LtCol, USAF, Chief Time Sensitive Targeting Cell, Operation Iraqi Freedon, Interviewed by Author December 7, 2004.

[17] http://www-cgi.cnn.com/TRANSCRIPTS/0303/20/bn.02.html

BIBLIOGRAPHY

Arkin, William M., Special Correspondent to the Washington Post, *The Myth of Military Lawyers,* URL ≤ http://www.washingtonpost.com/ac2/wpdyn?pagename=article&node=&contentId=A445 46-2001Dec14&notFound=true>. Accessed 15 October 2004.

Clausewitz, Carl, Von, *On War,* Indexed and Translated by Howard, Michael and Paret, Peter, 1976, Princeton University Press.

Cronican, John G. Jr., Colonel**, USAF,** *Centralized Control and Decentralized Execution,* Air University Review, September 5, 2001, URL: < http://www.airpower.maxwell.af.mil/airchronicles/aureview/1981/jan-feb/cronican.htm>. Accessed 24 October 2005.

Danskine, William B., Major, USAF, *Time-Sensitive Targeting Model,* URL: < http://www.airpower.maxwell.af.mil/airchronicles/cc/Danskine.html>. Accessed 30 November 2004.

Department of Defense, Joint Publication 3.0; URL: < http://www.dtic.mil/doctrine/>. Accessed 15 October 2004.

Grant, Rebecca, Correspondent, Journal Of The Air Force Association, *The Redefinition of Strategic Airpower, October 2003, URL: < http://www.afa.org/magazine/oct2003/1003strategic.asp*>. Accessed 29 Oct 2004.

Hersh, Seymour M., Correspondent, The New Yorker, *The Gray Zone*, URL: < http://www.cs.umass.edu/~immerman/play/GrayZone.html>. Accessed 30 Sep 2004.

Hillaker, Harry, Correspondent to Code One Magazine, *Tribute To John R. Boyd,* Code One Magazine, July 1997, Lockheed Martin Aeronautics Company, URL: < http://www.codeonemagazine.com/archives/1997/articles/jul_97/july2a_97.html>. Accessed 15 October 2004.

Hura, Myron., McLeod, Gary., Mesic, Richard., Sauer, Philip., Jacobs, Jody., Norton, Daniel., Hamilton, Thomas, *Enhancing Dynamic Command and Control of Air Operations Against Time Critical Targets*, RAND Corporation Publication, 2002, URL: < http://www.rand.org/publications/MR/MR1496/>. Accessed 10 October 2004.

Lazarski, Anthony J., Lt Col, USAF, *Legal Implications of the Uninhabited Combat Aerial Vehicles*, Aerospace Power Journal, Summer 2002, URL: <

http://www.airpower.maxwell.af.mil/airchronicles/apj/apj02/sum02/lazarski.html#lazarski>. Accessed 15 October 2004.

Orban, Brian, TSgt, USAF, *Thunder in the Desert, Time sensitive targeting builds flexibility in combat*, The Journal of the Air Force C4 Community, URL: < http://public.afca.af.mil/Intercom/2003/june/09.html>. Accessed 12 Oct 2005.

Prina, L. Edgar, Editor Emeritus to navy league of the United States, *Air War Kosovo, Lessons Learned and Relearned*, URL: < http://www.navyleague.org/seapower/air_war_kosovo.htm>. Accessed 21 Oct 2004.

Thirty dead in Baghdad market strike, Spacewar.com, URL: < http://www.spacewar.com/2003-a/030328231429.y0zzxeci.html>. Accessed 19 Oct 2004.

United States Central Command, *OIF By the Numbers*, URL: < http://www.globalsecurity.org/military/library/report/2003/uscentaf_oif_report_30apr2003.pdf>. Accessed 15 October 2005.

United States Government Accounting Office, *Operation Desert Storm: Operation Desert Storm Air War*, URL: < http://www.fas.org/man/gao/pem96010.htm>. Accessed 12 October 2005.

BIBLIOGRAPHY

Alsace, Juan A. "In Search of Monsters to Destroy: American Empire in the New Millennium." *Parameters.* U.S. Army War College Quarterly, Vol XXXIII, No 3., Carlisle, Pennsylvania, Autumn 2003.

Benfield, Darrell C., Major, USMC. Action Officer, J-5 Section, U.S. Pacific Command, 2004-2005. Unclassified, electronic interview by author, 15 December 2004.

Blair, David. "How to Defeat the United States: The Operational Military Effects of the Proliferation of Weapons of Precise Destruction." in *Fighting Proliferation: New Concerns for the Nineties.* ed Henry Sokolski., The Nonproliferation Policy Education Center. Washington, D. C. Maxwell Air Force Base, Alabama: Air University Press, 1996.

Bush, George W., President of the United States. *The National Security Strategy of the United States of America.* N.p., 2002.

Cahlink, George. "Move 'Em Out: The Pentagon prepares to reposition tens of thousands of overseas troops and civilians." *Government Executive.* October 15, 2004. URL: < http://www.govexec.com/features/1004-15/1004-15s2.htm>. Accessed 30 November 2004.

Cordesman, Anthony H. *The Gulf and Transition. US Policy Ten Years After the Gulf War: The Challenge of Providing USCENTCOM and US Power Projection Forces with Adequate Capabilities.* (Arleigh A. Burke Chair in Strategy, Center for Strategic and International Studies, Washington, DC), URL: <http://www.csis.org/gulf/reports/subforces.pdf>. Accessed 3 October 2004.

Cortes, Lorenzo. "FY '06 Planning Should Feature Help For Marine Corps, CNO Says." Defense Daily, 8 September 2004. URL: <http://ebird.afis.osd.mil/cgi-bin/ebird/displaydata.pl?Requested=/ebfiles/s20040908318500>. Accessed 8 September 2004.

Defense Security Cooperation Agency. *Expanded IMET,* 28 February 2005. URL: <http://www.dsca.osd.mil/programs/eimet/eimet_default.htm>. Accessed 28 February 2005.

Eisman, Dale. "The Navy's Changing Tide, Part 2: Will 'Sea Base" Idea Float? The Virginian –Pilot, 8 March 2005. URL: <http://ebird.afis.osd.mil/cgi-bin/ebird/displaydata.pl?Requested=/ebfiles/e20050308356414.html>. Accessed 8 March 2005.

Esplin, Jayson S. Maj, USAF. "Broadening the Concept of Expeditionary Air Forces for a New Millennium of Uncertainty." Unpublished Paper. School of Advanced Warfighting, U.S. Marine Corps Command and Staff College. Quantico, Virginia, 1999.

Federation of American Scientists. *US International Security Assistance Education and Training*, 28 February 2005. URL: <http://www.fas.org/asmp/campaigns/training.html>. Accessed 28 February 2005.

Grossman, David A. LtCol, US Army Ret. *On Killing.* New York: Little, Brown and Company, 1996.

Havens, Michael Lieutenant Commander, USN; Melso, Michael, Major, USMC; McNerney, Michael, Major, USAF; and Peney, Radko, Lieutenant, Bulgarian Navy. "Joint Seabasing: A Force Multiplier for Joint and Coalition Operations." Unpublished Paper. Joint and Combined Warfighting School-Intermediate, Class #04-3. Joint Forces Staff College. Norfolk, Virginia, 2004.

Hummer, Steven. Maj, USMC. "Forward Deployment and the Human Factor as the Marine Corps enters the Twenty-First Century." Unpublished Paper. School of Advanced Warfighting. U.S. Marine Corps Command and Staff College. Quantico, Virginia, 1992.

Johnson, W.F. Maj, USMC. "Operational Maneuver from the Sea: A Logistical Perspective." Unpublished Paper. School of Advanced Warfighting. U.S. Marine Corps Command and Staff College. Quantico, Virginia, 1992.

Krepinevich, Andrew, Barry Watts, & Robert Work. *Meeting the Anti-Access and Area-Denial Challenge.* Washington, DC: Center for Strategic and Budgetary Assessments, 2003. URL: <http://www.csbaonline.org/4Publications/Archive/R.20030520.Meeting_the_Anti-A/R.20030520.Meeting_the_Anti-A.pdf>. Accessed 28 February 2005.

Ladd, Maj. "Being Smarter about Getting Smaller." Unpublished Paper. School of Advanced Warfighting. U.S. Marine Corps Command and Staff College. Quantico, Virginia, 1991.

Marine Corps Doctrinal Publication (MCDP) 6. *Command and Control.* Washington, DC: Department of the Navy, 1996.

Marine Corps Doctrinal Publication (MCDP) 1. *Warfighting.* Washington, DC: Department of the Navy, 1997.

Melso, Mike. Maj, USMC. "Seabasing Concepts." Unpublished paper. Master's Thesis, U.S. Marine Corps Command and Staff College. Quantico, Virginia, 2004.

Paik, Jin-Hyun. "Post-Reunification Korea: The Role of Multilateralism." PacNet Newsletter #18, Center for Strategic and International Studies (CSIS). 1 May 1998. URL: <http://www.csis.org/pacfor/pac1898.html>. Accessed 8 March 2005.

"Rumsfeld Says Navy Can Operate With Fewer Carrier Groups." *Defense Today*, September 24, 2004. URL: <http://ebird.afis.osd.mil/cgi-

bin/ebird/displaydata.pl?Requested=/ebfiles/e20040924323561.html>. Accessed 24
September 2004.

Rumsfeld, Donald H. "Positioning Our Military For A Rapidly Changing World." Special to
   The Times, September 23, 2004. URL: < http://ebird.afis.osd.mil/cgi-
   bin/ebird/displaydata.pl?Requested=/ebfiles/e20040924323557.html>. Accessed 23
   September 2004.

"U.S. To Cut Number Of Overseas Bases." *Los Angeles Times*, September 24, 2004. URL: <
   http://ebird.afis.osd.mil/cgi-
   bin/ebird/displaydata.pl?Requested=/ebfiles/e20040924323499.html >. Accessed 24
   September 2004.

"U.S. To Close 35 Percent Of Overseas Bases." *New York Times on the Web*, 23 September
   2004. URL: <http://ebird.afis.osd.mil/cgi-
   bin/ebird/displaydata.pl?Requested=/ebfiles/e20040923323310.html>. Accessed 23
   September 2004.